Bath Time

Written by
Allison Holness

Illustrated by
Dan Cooper

AuthorHouse™
1663 Liberty Drive
Bloomington, IN 47403
www.authorhouse.com
Phone: 833-262-8899

This book is printed on acid-free paper.

ISBN: 978-1-4389-8283-0 (sc)
ISBN: 978-1-4685-8692-3 (e)

Print information available on the last page.

Published by AuthorHouse 02/23/2021

authorHOUSE®

To my beautiful grandchildren

who make unconditional love such a delightful reality!

Every evening, right after supper and before bedtime, little Obi has his bath.

At that time, his mother says, "Now Obi, you have had a long day, and now it's time for you to get nice and clean!"

Then she takes him upstairs, into the bathroom, and fills his little bathtub with warm water.

She puts in two drops of bath oil, one bath cube, and all of Obi's bath toys: a yellow duck; two fishes, one blue and one pink; a green turtle; and an orange frog.

Then, very gently, she helps Obi to brush his teeth, all four of them.

Next, she takes off his clothes and puts him into his bathtub.

Gently, she washes his face, behind his ears, his neck, his arms, his hands, and his fingers.

She washes the rest of his body, including his tummy, his back, his legs, his feet, and his toes.

And for a little while, Obi plays with his bath toys: a yellow duck; two fishes, one blue and one pink; a green turtle; and an orange frog.

Just about that time, Obi's mother leans over close to his ear and speaks ever so softly and sweetly.

"I am so proud of you, Obi. You are a wonderful boy, so smart and strong. I love you very much."

Then she kisses Obi gently on one wet cheek, lifts him out of his tub, and wraps him in a soft, fluffy towel.

And while she is carrying Obi to his bedroom, wrapped in his soft, fluffy towel, Obi's mother speaks softly to him.

"I am so proud of you, Obi. You are a wonderful boy, so smart and strong. I love you very much."

The End

Printed in the United States
by Baker & Taylor Publisher Services